Sipping Tea

Sipping Tea
for the Spirit

Carolyn R. Hobbs

Orange Universe Press
OrangeUniverse10@yahoo.com
501.765.1480

ISBN 978-0-9972312-2-9

Book and cover design: H. K. Stewart

Cover photograph: The tea cup belonged to John
David Brison, Jr., and the framed photograph
shows Rose Drake (seated in front), John David
Brison (on left holding his granddaughter),
John's son Gene Brison, and Gene's wife.

Printed in the United States of America

This book is printed on archival-quality paper that
meets requirements of the American National
Standard for Information Sciences, Permanence of
Paper, Printed Library Materials, ANSI Z39.48-1984.

Dedication

*T*his book is dedicated to my lovely parents and siblings.

This book is dedicated to all of the great youth and families who have crossed my path and lit my heart.

This book is dedicated to the memory of my great-great-grandmother, Rose Drake.

This book is dedicated to all of the Brison, Bryson family and their descendants.

This book is dedicated to the Hobbs, Jones,
Kilgore, Davis, and Covington families—
my maternal and paternal grandparents'
descendants.

This book is dedicated to all of my teachers,
professors, mentors, and neighbors who
assisted in directing my path.

This book is dedicated to Mary Brister, Marilyn
Bracy, and Calvin Coleman, my friends
since grade school.

This book is dedicated to Deborah Thompson
for providing support and positive energy.

This book is dedicated also to providing insight,
support, and hope to all who read it.

Table of Contents

Acknowledgements

9

$\mathcal{I}$ want to express my gratitude to my mother, Lula Hobbs, for desiring to read positive material about the lives of African Americans. I am grateful to my father, Dr. Antony O. (A. O.) Hobbs, for believing in me through the writing process. I thank my godfather, Dr. Lorenzo Thompson, Robert Hawkins (Dr. Bob), and Alma Jones for always being there for me. I thank Shelby Porter for encouragement, typing, and proofreading; Jordan Hobbs for his support and enthusiasm; Antony Hobbs II and Marcia Hobbs for allowing me to write about Antony Hobbs III; Marshall Hobbs for allowing me to write his story; Elvisto Hobbs for living his dream of living in Montana on an Indian Reservation. I also want to extend appreciation to Bonita Hobbs for professional proofreading and editing, and to Mary Debra Clifford for reviewing and copy editing. I also would like to extend a very special thank you to the late Mrs. Shirley Armstrong, my high school English teacher from Marianna, Arkansas, who encouraged me to write. I would like to thank the late Mrs. Beulah Flowers, a great teacher from Stamps, Arkansas, who encouraged Dr. Maya Angelou to speak again; she introduced her to poetic literature, which enabled her to become a great poet. Dr. Angelou inspired Oprah Winfrey, and Oprah continually inspires me. A special thanks to Dr. Martha Flowers, MD, of Pine Bluff, Arkansas, for allowing me to use her grandmother's name, Mrs. Beulah Flowers.

This book is small; however, the human experiences are enormous and invaluable. It's my desire that this book comes alive in your heart, mind, and spirit. I hope you will become blissfully grateful, for I am blissfully grateful that the title for this book came to me in 2011.

Introduction

This book consists of short stories about events and people who I have observed growing up in the South. Some of the names were changed due to confidentially. There were special role models in my life who contributed to making these stories come alive. My life has been special because of the people I have encountered.

Growing up in the South had a major impact on my life. Growing up in Arkansas has had its rewards; however, there have been many challenges along the way.

I realize that I have a choice to focus on the positive or the negative aspects of life. I decided to focus on the positive, creating gratefulness. I write this book with a prevailing spirit that is blissfully grateful.

Aunt Alma and Grandma

Aunt Alma's stories about her grandmother's experience in slavery allowed me to have an insight into slavery. I felt Aunt Alma allowed me to be a witness to slavery by reporting stories about Grandma, who was my great-great-grandmother. Grandma was raped and impregnated with the slavemaster's child when she was twelve years old. The child born from the rape was Aunt Alma's father. His name was John David Brison.

Aunt Alma was my hero. She was small in stature, but big in heart. She represented strength, boldness, faith, and love. The first events I remember about my aunt were when I was a child around four years old. She would wake up early and make our breakfast. Then she would eagerly prepare our lunch and walk a mile to carry my younger brother and me to Ms. Robinson's house. Ms. Robinson was one of Aunt Alma's best friends. She was kind and treated us as if we were special jewels.

Aunt Alma would carry my younger brother in her arms and hold my hand. I was four, and my younger brother was two years old. Aunt Alma would walk another two miles to work as a maid. She would clean house and cook all day. After work, Aunt Alma would then walk three miles and retrieve us from Ms. Robinson.

After we arrived home, she would prepare a big luxurious dinner for us consisting of some of my favorites, such as smothered chicken, mashed potatoes, greens, cornbread, tomatoes, onions, and chocolate cake. Her nights would consist of canning vegetables out of her fertile garden, sewing, and storytelling.

She loved telling us stories about Grandma, her grandmother, my great-great-grandmother. Grandma, as Aunt Alma so lovely called her, had

14

assisted in rearing her. Aunt Alma's mother had passed away when she was a child. The stories about Grandma's experiences in slavery always saddened me.

Grandma was born a slave in Mississippi and named Rose Drake. She spoke of her experiences daily to Aunt Alma and her siblings. Grandma told the stories about how she cooked and cleaned the slavemaster's home. She worked from sun up to sun down, seven days a week. All of the stories were sad. It appeared that talking about slavery assisted Grandmother Rose in coming out of the trauma and shock of the inhumane treatment of slavery.

One of the stories that Grandma told Aunt Alma centered on a little slave girl. She lived with Grandma in a little shack near the slavemaster's Big House. The slavemaster was her father. The slavemaster's wife resented her. She would give the little girl tasks impossible to complete. The slavemaster's wife would yell at her and pull some of her long braids out of her head.

The stories about slavery were devastating. Grandma Rose was twelve years old when slavery ended. Her father had been sold off to another plantation when she was a small child. Grandma told Aunt Alma she only remembers waking up in the the slavemaster's house. After slavery ended, Grandma's father, David Drake, returned to the plantation to get his daughter. She was around twelve years old and pregnant with the slavemaster's child. Her dad was very disappointed that she was pregnant, but was very relieved that she had not been sold off to someone in another state. Her mother had been sold to someone in Texas.

16

Grandma's father carried her to where he lived, Kosciusko, Mississippi. Grandmother Rose's bi-racial baby was born there. She named him John David Brison. John Brison was the slavemaster's name. David was her father's first name. Grandma's father assisted her in rearing her son.

John David Brison grew up to be a successful farmer. He owned two farms, one in Mississippi and one in Arkansas. He was the father of thirteen children. One of his daughters was my grandmother, Elnora Brison Jones. Grandmother Nora passed away when my mother was three years old. Aunt Alma promised Grandma Nora that she would help raise her children. Grandmother Nora told Aunt

Alma that she wanted her children raised well. Aunt Alma assisted in raising Grandmother Nora's children, her grandchildren, great-grandchild, and great-great-grandchildren.

Generation after generation will know the story about Grandma Rose's plight in slavery. Grandma lived to be almost 100 years old. She passed away in 1945. My mother remembers her rocking in her rocking chair at Aunt Alma's house. After her son (Papa) passed away, she lived with Aunt Alma. Aunt Alma shared her stories with a great love and respect.

Aunt Alma never complained about anything. She only had one white uniform that she wore to work every day. She washed it daily. She never complained about helping us. She always made us feel important. There were times my mother was ill and we would live with her. Aunt Alma was kind, and she helped everyone. She would share the vegetables from her garden and eggs from her chickens. She was a great cook. If she thought my parents were operating on a low budget, she would cook dinners and bring them to our house. Aunt Alma continued to help people in her eighties and nineties.

When I reminisce about Aunt Alma and how she shared the stories of the legacy of Grandma's life, I am exceptionally grateful. I am also grateful that my aunt discussed slavery and emancipation. After slavery, Grandma Rose devoted her life to rearing her son and grandchildren and healing the sick.

Grandma was a natural healer and a midwife. The local doctor would often tell families, when he had used all of his medical science, that they should seek the help of Grandma Rose or contact the funeral home. Grandma Rose had the ability to go to the forest and find herbs and plants that would often heal people. Grandma also assisted in helping people during a tuberculosis epidemic, and she never contracted it herself.

The thought of my great-great-grandmother as a human slave is appalling. However, the thought of Aunt Alma and Grandma's amazing abilities to help others are grand reflections I see in my cup, when sipping tea for my spirit.

*Rose Drake, a former slave and my
great-great-grandmother.*

20

Arlene Brison, my great-grandmother. She was married to John David Brison, who was the son of Rose Drake, my great-great-grandmother.

*Elnora Brison, my grandmother. She was
the daughter of Arlene and John David Brison
and the granddaughter of Rose Drake.*

22

*Page one of a three-page letter from Elnora
(my grandmother) to her sister Alma.*

letter last week an dilent
never finish it. so
grandmother is at Bill
John. Albert carried
her yesterday Alma I
did not feel like carrying
her so I tryed my best
to get her to stay another
week with me. she has
did very well since she
been here. so she say
she is going over to papa
an from their home.
well I did injoy her when
she were here. Alma
I wish you could get
some greens they sure
is fine. now I want
you to come an stay
all night with me

Page two of the letter.

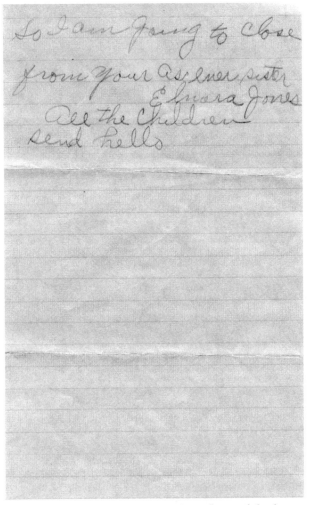

24

Page three of the letter.

*The letter's envelope showing the
October 10, 1939, postmark.*   25

Dark Shadows

*D*uring the Freedom of Choice Plan, my father, with great resistance from my mother, decided to send my two brothers and me to a white school in Marianna, Arkansas, where I was born. (According to Wikipedia, Freedom of Choice, also Free Transfer, was the name given to a number of plans developed in the U. S. during 1965–1970 that were aimed at the integration of public schools. In practice, most schools remained segregated, with only a small minority of black students choosing to attend a white school and no white students choosing a black school.[1])

I was starting the third grade when I was sent to Whitten Elementary School, which had been segregated in the past. We were faced with hatred and racism. Marianna is a small town approximately fifty-five miles west of Memphis, Tennessee. Memphis is where the Rev. Dr. Martin Luther King, Jr., was assassinated. I remember the day he was assassinated. I remember my mother crying the same way she did when my great grandmother, Mama Lula, died. Mama Lula was my mother's paternal grandmother. She assisted in rearing her.

The first year at the new school, we were attacked by bullies. We had to fight or be hit with rocks and bottles. Fighting was not a problem for us because we had recently moved from my grandfather's farm. My brothers and I would always have dirt wars after my grandfather's fields were freshly plowed. I was larger than my younger brothers. My older brother, Tony, had trained me to be very tough. He always chose me to be on his football team as opposed to my younger brothers. We used the same tactics that we used in the dirt wars; however, instead of dirt, we used rocks to fight the boys. The white boys not only bullied us, but attacked us every evening after school. The boys eventually stopped attacking us. There were two other fights with two girls who called me a nigger.

Upon entering the school where only white children had been able to attend, I went from making above average grades to barely passing. My third grade white teacher had low expectations of me. There were not any black teachers there.

My mother would dress me beautifully in bright pastel dresses and matching hair bows. My mother wanted desperately to show that I was as good as the little white girls. I was very frightened; however, I coped the best I could with the challenges.

29

My fourth grade year, I met Mallory Williams. We became friends very easily. She loved her black maid and her maid's children. Mallory and I had a common love for *Dark Shadows*. *Dark Shadows* was an interesting, popular horror show at that time. We would sit next to each other and talk about *Dark Shadows*. We would be punished for talking too much in class. Our punishment would consist of sitting in the hall. Sitting in the hall was a punishment that was aimed at embarrassing the students, but we were never embarrassed. We loved sitting outside the class in the hallway. Mallory and I held hands and continued to talk about *Dark Shadows*. Mallory and I loved each other unconditionally. Picture a small white girl with blonde hair and blue eyes comforting a small black girl with fuzzy braids and brown eyes.

When I reflect on the unconditional love that Mallory and I shared with each other and the profound difference it made in my life, it is powerful as I sip tea for my spirit.

30

1. Green v. County School Board, 391 U.S. 430 (1968). Allen, Jody and Daugherty, Brian. "Recovering a 'Lost' Story Using Oral History: The United States Supreme Court's Historic Green v. New Kent County, Virginia, Decision," *Oral History Review.* Vol. 3, issue 2, 25-45 (June 2006).

Antony Hobbs III (The Gentle Giant)

On January 2, 2008, Antony passed out on the basketball court and never regained consciousness. There was not a defibrillator in the gym. It was established that if there had been one available; he could have possibly been revived.

Antony physically left us that day, but his spirit lives forever and his death has saved countless lives. Antony's passing touched the hearts of the people in the State of Arkansas and across the nation.

His teachers, principal, and friends all stated that he was bigger than life. He stood at 6'9" and always had a big smile. At his memorial services, hundreds of people attended. Many dignitaries were present. The principal of the school stated that Antony would ask students randomly if they had done their homework. If they said yes, he would say, "Prove it. Let me see it."

Antony lives forever through several initiatives and scholarships. The General Assembly of the State of Arkansas established and enacted Act 496 of 2009, the Antony Hobbs III Act. The Act created school-based automated external defibrillators and cardiopulmonary resuscitation programs. The Act required each school campus to have an automated external defibrillator.

The Antony Hobbs Project was another profound initiative. The Hobbs Project was initiated by Dr. Jimmy Tucker of Arkansas Specialty Orthopedic, St. Vincent Hospital, and Embeds, Inc. of Little Rock, one of America's largest suppliers of automated external defibrillators and training. To launch the program, each organization made major donations to provide a defibrillator and special training to every high school in the Little Rock School District.[2]

Arkansas Specialties also sponsors the Antony Hobbs Award. It is given every year to a high school

32

student and is promoted on Little Rock TV Channel Seven. The award is based on team spirit.[3]

Antony was my oldest brother's youngest son and my dad and brother's namesake. He enjoyed the time he spent with his dad in the gym and fishing and camping. He preferred that to hanging out with his peers. They were buddies, best friends. He simply adored his mother, and his mother adored him. He passionately loved his only sister. Not long after Antony passed, his parents received information that the reserve unit of his older brother, Sergeant Toriano Hobbs, was going to be activated. Tori stated later that Antony's spirit protected him in the Iraq War.

Antony was an awesome son, grandson, brother, nephew, cousin, friend, and athlete. All of the students and staff loved him at Parkview High School. Antony loved to go to church with his parents and younger sister. He was a great basketball player, not just because of his skills on the court, but because he embraced sportsmanship.

When I reflect on Antony, who was a true hero, I reflect on how the lives of athletes, an umpire, and spectators have been saved.[4]

33

Antony loved and was loved. I am in awe of my nephew, "A Powerful Gentle Giant." I feel his profound love when sipping tea for my spirit.

34

1. http://www.arkleg.state.ar.../Acts/2009/public/acts 496 .pdf
2. http://www.emedamerica.com/the-company-hobs project
3. http://www.katv.com
4. www.katv.com

Empowerment of Little Rock Youth

I graduated from college with a degree in criminal justice in 1981. I remember when we were studying street gangs' activity. The professor proudly announced to us that gangs are in the larger cities, like L.A. and Chicago. There are not any gangs in Little Rock.

After I graduated from college, a female professor and mentor encouraged me to take my knowledge and education back to my community. I gained valuable work experience in Houston, Texas, and returned home to Little Rock, Arkansas. My first job upon returning home was at an emergency shelter for youth. Some of the youth had been badly abused. Other youth in the shelter consisted of runaways, throw-aways, homeless, and some were devil worshipers. I saw children in great pain. We were trained to not take their behavior personally. We collaborated with many agencies to assist the youth in becoming stable. It felt as if I had a knife in my heart daily, seeing the children hurting so badly.

36

After about four years at the shelter, I begin to see a new trend with our youth. We assisted many children across the state of Arkansas. I started to see the youth slowly turn toward gang affiliations. I left the youth shelter after six years. I took a position as a Youth Gang Intervention Specialist. I was the lone female who assisted in training ten male Gang Intervention Specialists. We provided gang prevention and intervention programs. The community-based initiatives consisted of after-school and summer programs. The programs were located in the most crime-ridden neighborhoods in Little Rock.

All of the staff that we trained were required to be on call 24 hours a day, seven days a week. We assisted the youth with transportation. We provided after-school enrichment and empowerment activities. We provided tutoring and assisted the parents in providing support in the schools. The participants received incentives for their hard work. We also provided parent support groups and grief counseling assistance after drive-by shootings. Then First Lady Hillary Rodham Clinton selected a group of youth from our program who were willing to say "no" to gang violence to take a trip to President Clinton's first Inauguration. The Inauguration experience inspired hope. One of the students I worked closely with, who had attended the Inauguration, completed high school and college.

37

I continued to work in prevention, intervention, and youth development. I accepted a position as executive director of a support center. Ironically, I did not apply for the job. The interim director, who was a therapist, called me and stated, "I found your resume on another staff member's desk, and I would like for you to interview for the executive director position. This center housed three gang intervention programs, two for males, and one for females. The support center also provided a prevention program for young children ages 6–12 and a support center for adults. The majority of the youth at the center came from low-education and high-poverty homes.

Another program that we provided was an in-house school program for expelled students. One student, who was suspended from the public schools for bad behavior, was assigned to the center. He later returned to the public school and became student of the month. The principal told me that student had become a role model at his high school.

One valuable tool we utilized was incentive points. Participants in the program at the support center received incentive points based on program participation, cooperation, attendance, social skills, leadership development, and academic improvement. The youth received enough points to take field trips. One of the first field trips was to Memphis, Tennessee, where they attended the Civil Rights Museum. They were astounded while touring the museum, which was the site of the Lorraine Hotel where Dr. Martin Luther King Jr. had been shot. Next, they visited a safe house. This house had been in use during the time of the

38

Underground Railroad. The youth were rewarded with a fun activity. They visited a theme park for their very first time. As a result of this, children who were once very hardened due to their environment were taken back to a sacred childhood dream. The excitment they displayed was astounding.

The youth, for their first time, checked into a luxurious hotel. It was the first time they had stayed overnight in a hotel. They dined in the hotel's restaurant. Their behavior was excellent in the restaurant. One of the restaurant guests asked me, "What church are you from? I've never seen such a large group of children behave so well in a restaurant. The group must be from a church group."

I then replied, "Oh no, this is a gang prevention and intervention program."

She was impressed. She stated that she would write a letter to the Mayor of Little Rock and tell him how well behaved the children were.

The lady we'd met that day was married. Her husband came and joined us in conversation. He introduced himself as John Brison. He stated he was from Mississippi. That startled me because my grandmother (Rose) was a former slave from

Mississippi. She was impregnated by the slavemaster. She named her son John Brison. She wanted her descendants to know their roots. The lady and I exchanged numbers, but once I returned to Little Rock, there was not any available time. I was busy, literally assisting with saving youth lives. I never had the opportunity to stay in contact them.

The youth stated that the field trips were a life-changing event for them. I remember vividly three brothers who attended. Their mother had passed away when they were very young. Their grandmother was a serious substance abuser. Their great-grandmother was an alcoholic, and these young men did not have a father figure in their lives. Their father was incarcerated while they were babies. The two older brothers were able to grasp the concept of our program. They did well. They became independent business owners. Sadly enough, the youngest brother didn't make it. He was brutally gunned down. My staff and I would go into the streets after drive-by shootings to ask the children to go home and not retaliate against the rival gangs. Those three young men were undoubtedly the most loving children I would ever meet.

40

The support center received needed support
with grants from the Robert Wood Johnson
Foundation, Annie Casey Foundation, City of
Little Rock, Pulaski County, State of Arkansas,
and the Federal Government. We also collaborated
with churches, Little Rock Police Department, and
the Little Rock School District. We provided training to the Little Rock Police Department and the
Little Rock School District on "Sensitivity while
Dealing with At-Risk Youths."   *41*

In one of my former positions, as a Youth
Intervention Specialist, I had assisted with gang
members in every area of the city. I would tell them
that I loved them all equally and that they were all
my children. The majority of the youth in every
gang sect respected me as if I were their mother.

One of my most heartfelt successes I witnessed was with Marco. He was best friends with
a gang leader. They both were participants in the
program. We were able to connect him with a mil-
itary recruiter. He passed the entry exam, and he
was able to join the Marines. After basic training,
he returned to the support center in full uniform.
I felt very proud about his ability to transition from

the life of a gang member to a great service man for our country. On 911, when the attack on the World Trade Center and the Pentagon took place, I admit I was once again afraid for his safety. I only felt relief when I spoke to him on the phone, and he said, "Mama Carolyn, don't worry about me, because I'm a soldier and I'm prepared to protect my country." He had become a courageous soldier.

I recently ran into Rodney, one of the former support center participants, at the supermarket. I had not seen him in many years. Rodney was once a vulnerable child who lived in the midst of one of the most gang-ridden neighborhoods in Little Rock. His mother stated that I was the first female mentor that Rodney had ever bonded with. I cried when I saw him. He was alive; he had a career and was married with five children. Several of his friends had been brutally killed during drive-by shootings.

The gang violence slowly ended. I am grateful. It was devastating to me to have a child in my program brutality gunned down in a drive-by shooting. During the height of the gang violence, HBO did a special documentary entitled, *Gang*

Banging in Little Rock. Currently, the children of Little Rock do not have to focus on what colors they are wearing. The children in Little Rock are safer. Those reflections are wondrous and glorious, when sipping tea for my spirit.

Halfway There

This story is dedicated to the late Dr. Charles Chastain. He was chairman of the Criminal Justice Department at the University of Arkansas at Little Rock. He strongly believed in rehabilitation. He believed in me and many other students.

My father came to me and asked me what was needed in the community. I knew immediately that there a need for transitional homes for women. I reflected on my history of coordinating strategies of success for youth in gangs. Research shows that one of the key factors that contributed to youth being at risk is that they were reared in homes that reflected poverty, low education, and poor parenting skills. I also observed the same factors while providing services for at-risk youth. I wanted to address core issues of females. I also wanted to provide enrichment and empowerment services to women. The H.E.L.P Home (Human Elevation Love Project) provided empowerment services to women in transition.

I grew up in a home where my mother was completely dedicated to her children. My mother often denied herself in order to give to us. However, that was not the case for many of the women who became residents at the transitional home.

46

The common themes among many of the residents were child abuse, poverty, and/or their father or mother being absent physically or mentally. There were females who came from influential homes. Some of the women reported that their spouses had persuaded them to try addictive drugs. There is one factor that all the women had in common. They appeared to have all felt unworthy.

(Research shows that "when one leaves incarceration or treatment center, the success rate is low if they do not have strong support systems.")

Whether it is a family member or organization, they will have better results if there is a support system available.

There was an urgent need to start transitional housing. The availability of transitional homes was limited for women. I was convinced if women were given a supportive living environment upon release from incarceration or a treatment center, they would have a better chance at striving. There were many women who would send me letters from prison requesting to be paroled to the home. I was startled at the large number of women incarcerated during that period.

The home was a safe haven for many women. The supportive environment of the home assisted the women in reintegration into society. The home provided the participants with life coaching, job assistance, substance abuse education, twelve-step meetings, mentors, clothes, and food. There was not any government funding available; therefore, they had to learn to become responsible quickly. It was rewarding to see the women who were in despair when entering the home begin to change and blossom.

Below are the stories of two of the residents who successfully transformed their lives at the Help Home. The names of the residents have been changed.

≈ ≈ ≈

Brandy was paroled from prison to the Help Home. She entered the home disgusted and dismayed. Brandy was an accountant prior to being incarcerated for writing hot checks. She wanted to find employment in the accounting field. She was a talented accountant. Her drug addiction had caused her to be dishonest and write hot checks. I suggested that she look in the mirror and see how beautiful and smart she was. I also suggested that she start at the bottom in a hotel chain that frequently hired our ladies. I told her she needed to be honest about her past. I recommended that she start at housekeeping and work her way up to management. She was promoted from housekeeping to front desk and from front desk to management. She's currently a manager of a hotel and receives respect and honor from the corporate office.

≈ ≈ ≈

Judy came from a treatment center located in a small town. There was not any place for her to go in that small town after treatment. The counselor at the treatment center was aware of the Help Home and suggested that Judy come and get some additional assistance. She followed all the rules of the home. She not only accepted my coaching, she appreciated and embraced it; she was transformed. She attained a job at a local hospital. She has continued to work there for many years.

49

Judy had a troubled teenage daughter. I was elated that her daughter safely completed high school. Judy's transformation allowed her the ability to assist her daughter. I witnessed dysfunctional cycles in family lives changing.

≈ ≈ ≈

It is magnificent when I reflect back on Brandy and Judy and numerous other women's lives that were transformed in the home. Their transformations had ripple effects and caused their children's lives to be transformed. Reflecting on the ripple effect of how the mother and child were transformed is phenomenal, when sipping tea for the spirit.

Marshall's Transformation

My brother called me and poured his heart out to me. It was in the middle of the night. He shared that he felt his life had become unmanageable. He asked me to send him money. I did not feel comfortable sending him money. Money had been sent to Marshall in the past. He had not used it responsibly; however, I agreed I would help him find placement in an excellent treatment center in Arkansas. During that time, I was an administrator of a support center. One of my mentors was the founder of an internationally known treatment center in Little Rock. Joe had developed amazing treatment methods.

Marshall Hobbs, my youngest brother, was greatly affected by my parents' divorce. My parents divorced when he was eleven years old. He dropped out of high school, left Arkansas, and moved to Michigan in his late teens.

Marshall arrived by bus to our hometown in Arkansas. He was not well. He visited one of his friends and discussed his malady. His friend's mother heard them discussing his malady and suggested he visit her church on his way home. Even though he was mildly intoxicated, he entered the church. The elders of the church knew Marshall. They prayed for him with love and concern.

My mother, with the help of a neighbor (Mama Nora), managed to get him to Little Rock. My mother first took him to my brother Elvisto's house. I asked a friend (nicknamed Doughnut) to make an intervention with Marshall. He is an alcohol and drug abuse counselor. He readily agreed to talk to him. He was a big, strong-statured guy and a former Arkansas Razorback. I think my skinny brother was afraid of him. My father and Doughnut assisted in getting him to my house. We continued the intervention. Marshall began his detox on my sofa. There were not any bed spaces available in any public detox centers nearby.

When I called the treatment center, they told me there was a six-month waiting list. I had to be very persuasive in order to get Marshall into the treatment center. The intake counselor finally agreed to allow my brother to come. He entered the treatment center with everything he owned in a sandwich bag. Marshall finished detoxing at the treatment center. One of the older counselors told me a light bulb came on for Marshall the last week he was there.

After he finished the thirty-day treatment program at that center, he left and entered a non-profit transitional living house. The roof was in need of repair. Marshall stated he "could look up through the ceiling and see the stars at night"; however, he was determined to stay for thirty days. In order for him to live there, he needed to find a job. The first job he could find was a position as a janitor. But things did not go well.

The work environment was unbearable. He was not accustomed to some of the harsh working environments in the south toward African Americans in comparison to his experiences in the north. He found another job as a janitor. The wages were low. On that job, he met a man who worked for a pest control service. Marshall asked the man if his company was hiring any new recruits. The technician told Marshall, no, the company was not hiring. My brother continued to work at that job. The job was not on the bus line. Transportation became an issue. He was fortunate to find a job closer.

He began working as a security officer. He crossed paths again with the same man from the pest control company. He asked if there were any job openings at that time, and the man answered, no. Marshall was later laid off from the agency where he was a security guard.

Losing this occupation forced Marshall to once again begin his rigorous search for employment. He found a part-time job working as a dishwasher for a church. Miraculously, once again, the same pest control man found his way back into my Marshall's life. The pest control technician was glad to see Marshall and told him the pest control company had just recently started recruiting new staff. Marshal was highly recommended by this "miracle man," for they had crossed paths three times and each time they met, Marshall was hard at work. This consistent work ethic impressed the technician. He was hired as a pest control technician trainee. Marshall loved his work immediately. The pest control company supplied him with training and a service truck. He traveled across rural Arkansas providing pest control service.

55

After working for that company for a year, Marshall began to recognize the lack of cultural diversity in Arkansas that he'd grown to love so well in the north. He longed for it. His supervisor had advised him not to be in certain areas at night.

One of Marshall's cousins asked him to relocate to Maryland. Marshall asked his company for a transfer and was transferred to Baltimore, Maryland.

In Baltimore, Marshall built a commercial route that was very promising for the company. After working very diligently, Marshall's route was given to another employee. He was reassigned to a residential route. The commercial routes paid more than the residential route.

He was disheartened by the company taking his route. He reluctantly resorted to seeking employment with another pest control company and was soon hired by that company. Marshall worked hard to establish a great route for the new company. The discomfort he'd experienced at the company prior to coming to this company was relived. The route that Marshall established was given to another white man. He was given a route that paid less money. Marshall remained determined. He searched again for another pest control company. Finally, he found employment with a company that treated him with integrity, dignity, and respect. He was given invaluable insight in the business aspect of running a company. He was also given elaborate and impressive clients. The clients included the managers of historical landmarks. The managers would report to the company of his excellent work.

Marshall gained confidence to start his own pest control business, Hobbs Professional Pest Control, where excellence is the norm. Marshall also invested in real estate.

Marshall has been alcohol free for over twenty-two years. Marshall helps others and gives back often. He has a love for travel and travels internationally. When I reflect on how Marshall prevailed through many difficult hardships and how many obstacles were faced and resolved, it causes me to be elated, when sipping tea for my spirit.

My Play Mamas

Mama Jean lived next door to my family on Izard Street in Little Rock. My mother, who was also named Lula Jean, and my sister, Bonita, and I loved to go sit and talk with Mama Jean on her big porch. We would talk and laugh on the porch for hours.

Mama Jean was a nurse. She was a very wise person. Mama Jean loved me dearly and always treated me special. She was a tall and beautiful lady who wore red lipstick and red nail polish. She would always state, "I will not go anywhere without my lipstick. If I just go down to my car, I am going to wear my lipstick." Her car was always parked on the street in front of her house. The importance of looking your best made a profound impact on me. I am known today by some as the lady who wears the red lipstick.

Mama Lummi Riley was my spiritual guide. She was also one of our neighbors who lived on Izard Street. When times were really difficult for me, I would ask her to pray for me. When she would pray for me, my life always changed in a positive manner. Her daughter, Shelby, has been one of my best friends since I was in the eighth grade. I would visit their house often. Mama Riley always made me feel exceptionally welcomed and treated me as if I were one of her daughters. Mamma Riley was a teacher. When she arrived home after school, she would share her wisdom about life's challenges.

Mama Riley had a special way that she showed me that I was worthy. When I became friends with her daughter, I gained two friends, Shelby and Mama Riley.

Mama Nora was a nurturing person. She always said that I was a nice girl. When I would come home from college, she would say, "You have gained some weight" as if I was happy to hear that. Then, she would say, "It show looks good on you baby."

I was in a horrific car accident when I was a young adult. I left the hospital and had to return to my mother's house. I could not take care of myself. Mama Nora would come by every day. She would allow my mother time to run errands. She would take care of me. She would assist in feeding me and giving me the bed pan. Her love and attention assisted me in regaining my strength. Mama Nora always made me feel worthy when I was in her presence.

Mama Hicks was employed at Yancey's, a local soul food restaurant. When I was in college, I would always go there to eat and talk. Mr. Kinard, the owner, would often allow me to have seconds if I wanted more food. I often needed someone positive to talk with during that time. I was elected to leadership positions in college. I was a member of the Chancellor and Dean Advisory Committee, and I was President of the Minority Student Association.

The Ku Klux Klan was allowed to rally on our campus. Several members of the Minority

Student Association and I, as president, met with the Chancellor. The Chancellor said that based on the Constitution, the Klan had the right to gather for a rally. Mama Hicks talked with me. She assured me that I had nothing to fear. She was right. There was not any violence. The Minority Student Association members witnessed the Klan's rallying. We watched while eating sweet potato pies under a tree. The sweet potato pie had been provided by a local black restaurant owner who was called "Say McIntosh." He was known for his world famous sweet potato pies. He was also known for his giving back to the community. His restaurant was named "Say McIntosh." We felt the pressure of the rally, but our stomachs were stuffed with sweet potato pies. Mama Hicks continues to serve love and joy at the restaurant. She greets me currently by saying, "Hello baby, how are you doing?" and that is incredible to me.

Mama Vera was vibrant, brilliant, and funny. Her daughter, Harriet, and I were friends and neighbors in Marianna, Arkansas. Mama Vera was a good listener. She treated me as if I were a member of her family. She asked me to eat meals with

62

them. I would always accept. When she married Harriet's stepfather, I was around thirteen years old. She selected me to be her maid of honor. She was full of wisdom and was always willing to share wisdom with me. Throughout my life, she was always there as a source of comfort.

Mother Annie Abrams is a very distinguished community activist and leader. She was involved in the desegregation of Central High School and renaming of a street to Honor Dr. Martin L. King. She gave me needed support when I became executive director of an agency whose mission was to support youth and families and to end destructive cycles. The agency faced many challenges. I called Mother Abrams. She invited me over to her home. She assisted me with strategies. She also supported the H.E.L.P. Home for women. She led a campaign at her church to provide needed donations to the H.E.L.P. Home. Her love, smile, and wisdom gave me strength during times of great controversies and challenges. Mother Abrams, a powerful and distinguished woman, took time for me. She amazed me with her sense of compassion for the community.

63

I reflect back on my life when I was a young child. I lived in the deep Delta of Arkansas, in an area named Black Swamp. They were ladies who exemplified humility, love, and trust. They were the ones who inspired me to believe that we are put here to love. Our neighbors across the road, Mrs. Elizabeth and Mr. Q., treated me and my siblings as if we were royalty. They treated us that way every time they saw us.

Mrs. Mattie enjoyed feeding us tea cakes and banana pudding. Mrs. Mattie had many children of her own; however, that never stopped her from sharing with us. Mrs. Vera would make sweet bread when her cupboard was low. I loved eating it with her children. There were ladies up and down our muddy roads that provided love, compassion, and kindness to us on a daily basis. I later perceived that spirit in other women and called them Play Mamas. My mother also provides that loving spirit to many.

As I sit and reflect on the great memories of the charismatic women I was fortunate to have in my life, I lovingly refer to them as my Play Mamas. I realize it was a privilege to have known such phenomenal women. I am amazed, as I sip tea for my spirit.

References

1. Green v. County School Board, 391 U.S. 430 (1968). Allen, Jody and Daugherty, Brian. "Recovering a 'Lost' Story Using Oral History: The United States Supreme Court's Historic Green v. New Kent County, Virginia, Decision," *Oral History Review*. Vol. 3, issue 2, 25-45 (June 2006).

2. http://www.arkleg.state.ar.../acts/2009/ public/acts 496.pdf

3. http://www.emedamerica.com/the-company-hobs project

4. http://www.katv.com

5. www.katv.com

About the Author

*C*arolyn Hobbs has more than fifteen years of experience providing services for at-risk children and their families. Carolyn has specialized in providing intervention services in some of the most horrific situations. Her love for children placed her in some of the most crime-ridden neighborhoods. It is her belief that all youth can thrive.

Carolyn has received the City of Little Rock Outstanding Citizens Award. She was the first

African American to serve two terms at Mount St. Mary Academy in Little Rock. Mount St. Mary Academy is the oldest catholic school west of the Mississippi River. The first term, she shared with an African American attorney. The attorney's schedule would not allow her to complete the appointment. Once again, Carolyn was faced with being the lone African American. The strong sense of respect she received from the Sisters of Mercy (R.S.M.) staff made it a warm experience. She was a member of the Little Rock Task Force.

She hosted *Dancing in the Light*, a television talk show on Comcast Cable in Little Rock for more than a year.

In Houston, Texas, Carolyn served as a Quality Assurance Administrator for more than 350 mental health clients. She also worked in research, assisting in a post-Katrina study jointly conducted for Harvard University and Princeton University.

Carolyn provides consulting, lecturing, training, and workshops in the areas of community development, grants writing, community program implementation, and evaluations. She also provides sensitivity training to teachers and police departments on dealing with at-risk youth.

Carolyn is a member of Delta Sigma Theta Sorority. She has a great love for nature and travel.